THE WINGS OF LOVE

Elsa Jauram

A MEMOIR

Edited by Astrid Wilson

New Generation Publishing

Published by New Generation Publishing in 2021

Second Edition

Paperback ISBN: 978-1-80031-252-4
Hardback ISBN: 978-1-80031-251-7
Ebook ISBN: 978-1-80031-086-5

www.newgeneration-publishing.com

 New Generation Publishing

My mother, 1934

Dedicated to

The Lord Jesus

Introduction

My mother, Elsa Emm, died in 2011 at the age of ninety-seven. Her long and eventful life spanned most of the twentieth century. It also reflected most of the devastating events of that century in Europe: the Russian Revolution, the Russian Civil War, the First World War and the Second World War. She was born in the Ukraine and then moved to Estonia, her native country.

As the Soviet tanks approached Estonia in 1944, she and the family were forced to flee. They escaped just in the nick of time, before the Iron Curtain came down and engulfed Estonia for almost fifty years. My mother eventually settled in Scotland but even in the apparently idyllic Scottish Highlands there were shocks awaiting her.

Before she died, she wrote an account of her life. Her memoir is uneven but certain sections are absolutely fascinating. They are fascinating because they contain vivid descriptions of much that happened in that period (1914 to 1935 and then at the end of World War Two.) and as such are, I think, important firsthand accounts of much that is accepted history. That is why I have decided to publish her memoir. I feel that her story has an interest that goes beyond that of the immediate family.

At first I was going to call this 'The Gates of Hell'. The Russian Revolution, the Russian Civil War, the Famine of the 1920s in the Ukraine and in Russia, World War Two: yes, the gates of hell had certainly opened. But then, when I thought about the tone of my mother's writing and the fact that my family survived despite the destruction and desolation, I thought, no, this is a story of victory, of victory in the face of unimaginable odds. My family was rescued, lifted up, taken out of the horror. And this happened again and again and again, from the flight from the blood bath that was Ukraine in 1921 to the resolution of a tragic situation in the Highlands of Scotland in 1950.

I feel that the hand of God was always present in her

story. In saying this, I do not mean she was somehow special and that she survived when millions of people did not. The atrocities of the Revolution, the barbarities of war, the horror of the concentration camp : there is nothing one can say. It is all beyond words, beyond language, beyond comprehension. In fact, in a way this is not about my mother and my family but about all who suffered in the terrible events of the last century.

The inspiration for the title came from the Christmas carol 'Hark the Herald Angels Sing'.

> 'Light and life to all he brings
> 'Risen with healing in his wings.'

The healing presence of Christ!

I chose the image of the dove returning to Noah because, after the deluge comes the calm. One can imagine the scene as, after the rain, it is now calm. Noah is staring out of the window. Then the dove arrives, a soft sweep of wings, perhaps a gentle cooing sound, I've done it, I've got it!

> *'and there, in its beak, was a freshly plucked olive leaf'*
> (Genesis 8,11)

It is only a tiny leaf but what it represents – hope, growth, renewal – is enormous.

Hope, growth, renewal: even after the most terrible of events, the potential is always there. My mother's life and my own long happy life are a witness to this. Even in the most difficult circumstances, a path will reveal itself. There will be opportunities, there will be helping hands.

God holds us as we suffer and he helps us up, he helps us to recover, he helps us to move on. There is always healing, there is always love. It is amazing. It is unbelievable.

Astrid Wilson
August 2018

Preface to Second Edition

'Light and life to all he brings,
'Risen with healing in his wings.'
('Hark the Herald Angels Sing')

The wings in the title of this book are Jesus' wings. There are three important religious experiences in my life in which the Lord Jesus has been especially close.

The first occurred when I was three years old. It was 1945. My family was Estonian and we were fleeing from the Soviets who had once again occupied Estonia. It was all too much for my grandmother and she died.

I had been sent away, but I had crept back to where it was all happening. I was in a dark corridor behind a closed door. Someone came along the corridor, a man, and he took hold of my hand and said,

'Come and say goodbye to your grandmother.'

The door opened. Suddenly there was a lot of light. I stepped into the room. Opposite me, propped up in a bed, lay my grandmother. At the foot of the bed were my mother and grandfather, both very agitated.

I wanted to run to my grandmother but something stopped me. I knew that something important was happening.

I became aware of Jesus' presence. It was just an awareness of a golden light and a feeling of overwhelming peace. I knew that my grandmother was going to be alright. I felt very calm.

Something passed between my grandmother and myself, and from then on, throughout my life, I was aware of her love coming down to me.

The other two experiences are very recent.

One happened only last year, in 2019. It was a vision of the Lord Jesus.

It was December 21 and I was sitting on the sofa in my sitting room. I was filling in a diary. I suffer from a psychosis for which I receive medication. I had reached a stage where I was analysing and over-analysing every thought that I had. My head began to spin and I felt confused.

I put the diary down, bowed my head and began to pray.

I became aware of Jesus' presence. There seemed to be a golden light around me and a sort of heat went through my heart.

First of all he said,

'Open your eyes.'

I opened them.

Then he said.

'Look up.'

I looked up.

Then he said,

'Astrid, you belong to me and you should stop writing this diary. We will always look after you and you should get a little dog.'

I said,

'Thank you, Lord Jesus.'

Then he was gone.

My Vicar, the Rev'd Chris Lee, believed that I had had a vision and I enacted this experience in front of the congregation at our church, St Saviour's, Hammersmith.

I was very deeply affected by this vision. At the beginning of Advent this year, I felt that people should know about the experience. I wrote a description of it in an article and I sent the article to all of the national newspapers. I received not one response.

I had already brought out a small edition of this book, The Wings of Love, which is a memoir written by my mother. There is a section towards the end of the book which portrays an unsettling experience that took place in the Highlands of Scotland in 1949.

I wrote an account of this in another newspaper article and I sent it to The Scotsman. I posted the article by email at 9 p.m. in the evening. The next morning the phone rang at 10 a.m. It was The Scotsman. They wanted to print the story.

This led me to think that I should bring out another edition of the book, this edition. The first edition had been very small and it was also presented in a very basic form. This time, I decided, I would use an upmarket self-publishing company and produce something smart and well-printed. I would also add some extra material.

Now I shall tell you about my third experience of the Lord Jesus. This happened only a couple of weeks ago. Once again, it was December 21 and once again I was sitting on the sofa in the sitting room.

I was not writing a diary but I was thinking about a lot of things. And again, as in the previous year, I was thinking about things that troubled me.

I picked up my Bible and opened it at random, hoping that there would be a message for me. It opened at Matthew 26.26.

'While they were eating, Jesus took a loaf of bread, and after blessing it he broke it, gave it to the disciples, and said, 'Take, eat; this is my body.' Then he took a cup, and after giving thanks he gave it to them saying, 'Drink from it, all of you; for this is my blood of the covenant, which is poured out for many for the forgiveness of sins.'

I took this to mean that I should spend time with Jesus. I put on a recording of The Messiah and began to pray and to reflect.

I reflected about a number of things. Some of my thoughts were about the events in this book. It is basically about the refugee experience and, of course, it is very sad. Others were about problems and difficulties that I was experiencing at the time.

Then, once again, I became aware of Jesus' presence. It was not like last year, but I knew that it was him. There was once again the sense of a golden light and also a feeling of warmth. I relaxed into his presence.

The problems I had been contemplating surfaced again. As I articulated them, a comforting answer would be given. I began to feel reassured but a certain unease of spirit remained.

Eventually I bowed my head and I began to pray. I said,

'Lord Jesus, I... I don't know what to say. I don't really know anything. I don't even know who I am.'

He replied,

'Wings is really you. It is what you have made of the material. Wings is who you are.'

Then he added,

'You are thinking about adding a lot of extra material. Don't. Just reprint it.'

X   X   X

What I have just described is of course very personal and intimate. It illustrates Jesus' love in the detail of one person's life.

What this book demonstrates is the exact opposite. This is a huge canvas, Europe and Russia in the throes of revolution and war, with famine thrown in for good measure.

My mother describes her own experience in this seething chaos but she is only a tiny dot on the canvas. Millions of people were involved and millions suffered and perished. They perished not just during the two world wars but in concentration camps, in deportations to Siberia, in prisons, in forests, in houses, in gardens.

Millions of people: shot on the edges of mass graves, gassed in concentration camps, hanged and shot in prisons, strangled in their own houses, shot in their own gardens.

So: what are we to take from this? What is our attitude to be? It looks as though Evil has won. Has it?

In 1 Corinthians 13.9 St Paul tells us, 'For we know only in part, and we prophesy only in part; but when the complete comes, the partial will come to an end'. In 2 Corinthians 4 .18 he expands on this: '... because we look not at what can be seen but at what cannot be seen; for what can be seen is temporary, but what cannot be seen is eternal.

'For we know that if the earthly tent we live in is

destroyed, we have a building from God, a house not made with hands, eternal in the heavens.'

What does this mean, with reference to this book? It means that the millions of victims who suffered in these horrors are now in heaven. Their suffering is over. They are in heaven and they are at home. They are at home with God. The Book of Revelation gives a very exact description of this:

'See, the home of God is among mortals,
He will dwell with them;
They will be his peoples,
And God himself will be with them;
He will wipe every tear from their eyes.
Death will be no more;
Mourning and crying and pain will be no more,
For the first things have passed away.'

(Rev.21.3)

What about the perpetrators of these horrors? They are dirt, dust, rubbish, rubble, swept away into nothingness.

So: where lies the victory?

As it was with Christ Jesus, a limp body on the most cruel of all execution systems, displayed in humiliation, having been flogged, derided, hated for years by the authorities.

Where lies the victory?

January 2021

War, Revolution, Famine

One

My dearest Astrid, Dagmar and Laura, I want to tell you my life story because it has been turbulent. I have lived through the First World War, the Russian Revolution, the Russian Civil War and the Second World War. And I must say that looking back I am rather surprised that I have survived all of them although at times it was rather grim.

I was born in Nikopol, Ukraine on the 8th of August 1914 when the First World War began. My father was born in Estonia and had come to Ukraine to work in the Manganese Ore Mines. At that time – 1906 – this manganese ore mine was quite small but now – 2006 – it is the largest in the world. He worked as an engineer because he could not find a good job in Estonia.

At that time, 1906, the Ukraine was Russian. My mother was born in the Caucasus in Vladikavkas and my father met her in a music shop where she worked. He was buying strings for his violin.

Life was so wonderful in the Ukraine. We lived in a big white house near the manganese mines, surrounded by a yellow acacia fence and a big white acacia tree grew near the house. The scent of its blossoms was wonderful. Father built a house in its branches and he used to play chess with the village school teacher. Sometimes they played all through the warm summer night and went to work without having slept at all.

There was a big orchard and an apricot garden and behind it stretched the endless Steppe. On one side of the house was a church with a belfry beside it. I liked to listen to the bells.

My first memory about my childhood was when I was about one year old and tried desperately to walk. I remember so clearly when I tried to grab the leg of the dining table and suddenly I stood on my legs. I was so thrilled that I had succeeded. Then I looked at the next table leg and wanted to make my first step in life to the next leg

– and the feeling of happiness was indescribable.

I had two brothers, Evald and Paul – Pavlik in Russian – but I did not play with them or other children but explored the immense Steppe and was fascinated by the great variety of flowers and their beauty. I also joined the village shepherd who took the cows of the village to the Steppe and also with our cows.

The First World War was raging – the traffic on the road passing our house was enormous.

My first childhood years passed very quietly. I spent them mostly in the wide mysterious Steppe – it was the flowers that attracted me, their beauty and their scent. I visited them every day, the whole long day.

I did not have any childhood friends. There was only a little boy, Prvo Kulikov, who sometimes came to play, but not for long because he sat on Father's beehives drumming his feet against the hive. The bees attacked him and stung him badly. Quite frequently I joined the village cow shepherd in the Steppe but this came also to a close because I tried to milk a cow using a little basket. The calf did not like this and kicked me with its hind legs so that I rolled down the slope and was badly hurt.

When I was three or four years old the Zeppelin aeroplane flew over our house one day and everybody ran to watch it. My father asked whether I could see it and my reply was 'yes, yes'. 'Where?' asked Father. 'There, under that bush!' Everybody laughed but I was very hurt and could never forget it.

In October 1917 the Revolution began. It did not affect me much, but the effect on the Russian people as a whole was enormous. Suddenly the Proletarians, that is the communists, formed the government and the Intelligentsia was completely annihilated.

The Cheka (Secret Police) was formed. I even remember the little songs sung by the anti-communists and I sang them occasionally.

'Little apple, where are you rolling to?
If the Cheka get you, you will never return.'

Another song was

'When Nicolas the silly fool was in government,
The bread cost only 5 kopecs.
Came the Soviets, bread was no longer available at all.'

Mother was horrified at hearing me singing these little songs. I was only four years old and had no idea how dangerous this was.

But the Revolution did affect my poor mother very badly. Suddenly we were not allowed to have any workers in the house and there was nobody to look after our little farm and animals. The women were not allowed to wear hats and fancy dresses. They had to do heavy work in the factories and streets.

On the whole any contact with an educated person was forbidden because they were 'enemies of the people'. Consequently, my parents could not longer associate with managers and families of the Manganese Mines.

Luckily Father came from a peasant family and had a good relationship with the workers. But nevertheless, he made a mistake. A manager (the financial director) had no children and his wife had asked Mother if I who was then 4-5 years old could stay with her, Olga Nikolaevna, for several days. It did not occur to my father that this would not be allowed. And so I went for five days to Olga Nikolaevna. After I returned my mother found that a large container filled with fat was stolen from the cellar which was situated outside the house. Apparently some workers did not like me staying with the family of a manager.

The same thing happened to us later when we gave shelter to the family of the mine's Direktor who was brutally executed for some reason and their house was set on fire. I remember very clearly when his wife and two girls, Marina and Tamara, and their nanny Antonina Petrovka came to us

13

begging for shelter. This was a cold dark night and we could not refuse. But we had to pay for this – we found our calf Sorka brutally killed in the Steppe. Only Sorka's beautiful skin was found by the shepherd. I was so upset.

The family of the Direktor of the mine consisted of his wife and two teenage daughters, Marina and Tamara. We did give shelter and food and Father could not refuse. And the result of this was that we suffered further reprisals.

One night when the Direktor's family slept in our house we heard loud knocking at our window shutters and loud voices. When we ignored these, the voices shouted louder and demanded entry. Father opened the door and a gang of drunken workmen armed with rifles stormed into the house and demanded money. One of them pushed Father to the wall of the hall and pressed his rifle against Father's chest.

Father said,

'Comrades, you know we have not been paid for some time, we have no money.'

Actually, he had some hidden behind the bricks of the Russian stove. We were terrified that at any moment the drunken worker could release the bullet and shoot Father. But the gang stormed into the house, opened all wardrobes and drawers and put the contents on sheets, pillows and bed linen.

I still remember how my body trembled and I was frightened to death. I saw my mother talk to one of the gang. And later she told me that she had told him to take the silver cutlery and the small samovar, it could be handy for him. But he refused, to her astonishment. Afterwards she said that even the worst criminal could have some goodness in him.

At last the gang left and Father could breathe freely. But we did not have enough blankets and pillows and suddenly Mother cried, where is Pavlik? We looked everywhere and Mother was weeping. But suddenly Pavlik crept from under the bed. But this was not the end. The gang returned and wanted more blankets.

Next morning I saw Father cutting some carpet material with scissors on the floor.

'What are you doing?' I asked.

'I am trying to sew a coat for your mother. She has none. The robbers took our clothes away. Your mother is very ill and must see a doctor.'

There was more trouble. We were told to vacate rooms for two families. One family consisted of two persons, one woman, Lida Soloveva and her young daughter. The woman was an active communist. She was always out on her red-brown horse and looting big houses. Her daughter often showed with pride the items that she stole.

The other family was a cobbler, Shubin and his wife. Father said that they had agreed to help each other when the looters came. But it proved later that he was afraid to show himself when we were in trouble and needed help.

My poor mother suffered most. She came from a large family that lived in the Caucasus. She got news that her parents who lived in Vladikavkas had been ordered to leave their home. *(Towards the end of WW1 all Russian nationals of foreign extraction were interned.)*

Her mother, Christine Schoch, was moved to a labour camp in Saratov on the Volga *(a notorious concentration camp)*. She died very soon of starvation.

Her father Herman was deported to Harbin in Siberia. He came back when the war ended, but then he was deported to the country of his origin, Germany. He lived in a cellar with another man. There were rats in the cellar and the other man bought some arsenic for the rats. He forgot to clean the knife.

When her father came home from a walk he used the knife to cut his bread. He died soon afterwards of arsenic poisoning.

My mother had many brothers and sisters scattered all over Russia. They were now 'enemies of the people' and my mother was not allowed to contact them. There was only one sister that she could write to, Laura. Laura had emigrated to the USA before the Revolution started.
Our life in the Ukraine got from bad to worse when the Revolution turned to Civil War and killing and looting

reached us. Our friends the Von Schiebenbergs, a German aristocratic family whose ancestors had been sent by Catherine the Great to the south of the Ukraine and who owned big areas of land and a large manor house, were brutally killed.

I liked their lovely garden with the great variety of fruit trees very much. Apart from peaches, apricots and grapes they had some mulberry trees for their sick to use. The ground around these trees was covered with delicious blackberries and how I loved them. They also had an interesting house with a large library and a large collection of butterflies, birds' eggs and stuffed birds.

And their manor house was partly burnt. The owner of the house was told to go to the wall and he was shot by his shepherd boy. Some members of the family managed to hide in their large pond and escape. One of them escaped by jumping into the toilet cesspit and holding down the lid with his hands and so saved his life.

Some people in a large villa, known to us, were also tortured and killed.

Mother's health was critical. Her hair was suddenly white and she lost some teeth.

My father was also in danger and had to hide in our maize and sunflower beds. My brothers and I had to take food for him and we were told the number of the row of maize plants and quite frequently we got confused with the rows and Father came at night and knocked gently on the shutters because he was hungry.

During these difficult times I suddenly got very ill. It started like this. My brother Pavlik and I had to guard our gate keeper's Burlyaeve's house since he and his wife were visiting some friends. After a while we were hungry and Pavlik went to Mother for some food. He appeared with a plate of fried potatoes. I could not eat them, I felt so sick. Pavlik had to call Mother and help me to bed. I had diphtheria. I had a very high temperature and at times I was unconscious. Unfortunately, there was no doctor in the village and the paramedic could not help me.

Luckily, my mother remembered to look into the medical box which her sister Margarita, who was married to a chemist, had sent her from Moscow. She found some capsules which the paramedic injected and gradually I felt better and I was saved from death.

But soon our life became even more dangerous because we were sheltering the family of the Direktor of the Manganese Ore Mine, Zhinomsky. Father was called to the Cheka with some other workers. At this meeting they were told from now on none of them were to have weapons, or they would be shot.

The Chairman of the meeting looked at Father and said,

'Jauram, you have a revolver, come, I shall search you.'

Father said,

'Comrade, I have no weapon at all.'

Quickly Father passed his revolver to the man sitting next to him. Thank goodness, Father got away with this. When he came home he buried his revolver in the garden and there it is, even to this day.

The men were also told at this meeting that Collective Agriculture is now the law and they would have to give their entire harvest to the government. If they kept some of it they would be shot.

Life got worse from day to day. Horrible stories of torture were going around. Our life was now unbearable. And Father had to do something about it. Now we could not even sleep at home since Zhinomsky's family depended on us. We had to sleep anywhere that we could find, away from the house. At times we even slept under bridges.

Sometimes we slept in an old barn in the field. And on one occasion we heard loud voices approaching us. We were so frightened and Father whispered to us to be very quiet. But the nanny of Zhinomsky's children still spoke so loudly and I was very frightened. Thank goodness the voices disappeared.

We could not trust anyone in the village or at the Manganese Ore Mines. There was only one Cossack family, the Muchins, that we could trust. The wife of the Cossack

Muchin was a great friend of Mother's and the Cossacks were all very anti-communist. During Stalin's time whole large communities of Cossacks were deported to Siberia to labour camps and died horrible deaths.

We were glad to have the Cossacks as friends. They were such a brave and colourful nation – beautiful songs, dances and tasty dishes.

Two

With our situation being so hopeless now, Father decided that we should escape to Estonia. He applied for a certificate to leave Russia and travel to Estonia. This was refused. They said Father could go since he was Estonian but not Mother or we children since we were Russian citizens.

But it was simply impossible for us to stay in the Ukraine. There was now not just a famine but a famine crisis. People were dying on the streets. Cases of cannibalism were reported.

But how could we escape this misery? Father had an idea, though a risky one. If it failed, all would be lost. He would be shot and we would be deported to the Gulag. He said that he would ask for a certificate for my mother to go to a health resort on the Black Sea. He would invent a fictitious name, one close to the word 'Estonia' which could later then be changed to 'Estonia'.

The uneducated clerks in the office would probably not notice that there was not such a resort at all. And indeed this is what Father did and he got away with it. But there of course was the danger that we could be in great trouble with the certificate if it was checked in the future.

The next problem was how to get a big enough wagon to accommodate five people and as much food as possible, also bed linen and of course food for two horses. We definitely had to get a wagon and horses as there was no regular transport of any kind or the possibility to buy anything at all. Not even matches, salt, sugar or any kind of food.

The Civil War was raging and the battles between the Reds and the Whites were quite fierce.

Father discussed this with his Cossack friends, the Muchins. They were very helpful and got him a big wagon which could stand up to the long journey from the Black Sea to Estonia. It would take many months and we would need good, strong horses.

And the Cossacks sold him two Uzbek horses. A brown horse which Father named Shamil. Shamil was the name of a famous Muslim hero who fought the Russians in the high mountains of the Caucasus and was very successful until he was finally defeated. The Russians admired him very much. The second horse was black and was named Mary by Father. I do not know why Father chose an English name.

Father made changes to the wagon such as a double bottom where he put all valuables, jewellery and silver, such as the cutlery that I still use. He took also his violin and Mother her guitar. I was surprised that Mother took a big box of Christmas decorations which she had got from her sister Margarita in Moscow because I did not think decorations were all that important and space in the wagon was limited.

We also had to take as much food as possible since it was not possible to buy anything. Fortunately Father had a good supply of honey from his bees. And ham from our pigs. He dried also a big supply of rusks. He had also a big bag of salt which he could exchange for food. A small samovar of silver to make tea or hot water. He had bought it in the Caucasus when he was working in the silver mines there.

At last all was ready but we children were not told where we were going, or when. Everything had to be kept secret.

We started our escape at the beginning of May 1921. The Muchin Cossacks received all our belongings that we left behind.

Father said it would be better if we were dressed as poor gypsies. Then the looters would leave us alone. For us children this 'trip' was fun. We had no idea about the dangers which were lurking everywhere around us.

Soon all three of us children got measles, whooping cough and mumps. Our temperatures were very high and we were sweating a lot. But Father did not allow us to stick our heads out of the wagon to get fresh air. He insisted this would make us feel worse.

The roads were very bad. Usually Father chose small country roads. When it rained the wagon wheels sank deeply into the soft mud and so we all had to get out of the wagon and help to push it. I was so sorry for Shamil and Mary but they were wonderful horses, so strong and willing to do their best.

When the weather was hot, a cloud of dust surrounded us all. I remember so vividly how the sweat was dripping from the poor horses.

Father walked beside them, his face also sweaty. His beard was now quite long. He wore a linen off white jacket and high Russian boots and now looked like a real gypsy.

Father avoided the towns because they were more dangerous than the country roads. But it was at a country road that we had a very frightening experience. Father had stopped to give the horses a chance to eat some grass along the road.

Suddenly two drunks with rifles stopped him and accused him of allowing the horses to graze on their field. This was not true at all because the horses were eating only the grass that was beside the road. Father explained, but they became more quarrelsome and said that, unless he gave the horses to them, they would shoot him in the woods beside the road. Father tried hard to pacify them but they dragged him into the wood and we lost sight of him.

Mother and we children were terrified. We thought this would be the end of us. We could not survive without Father. Mother was desperately praying.

About half an hour later, which seemed an eternity to us, Father appeared from the wood, white as a sheet. He said he had fallen to his knees and begged them with tears,

'Please, comrades, do not shoot me. What are my three children and wife going to do? They are innocent and will die in the end. I am sure you have children yourselves and that you have a kind heart.'

This seemed to have an effect.

'OK,' they said, 'you can go.'

June and July (1921) were very hot months and there was a drought. The vegetation along the road was covered with a thick layer of dust. I can clearly remember the cherry trees that grew beside the road. In the evening Father used to stop at large villages where he could get information about the fighting going on between the Reds and the Whites.

The name Machno was often mentioned. Machno was a Ukrainian military leader who at times fought the communists and at other times the Whites. He was very good looking and the Ukranian girls used to sing, ' I would marry neither Lenin nor Trotsky but Machno the Ukranian.' I am surprised that, young as I was, I still remember this song.

We were very glad when we met another Estonian family who was also escaping from the Civil War. Their name was Vaino. We children were especially glad that now we had the company of two girls of my own age. But Father and Mr Vaino could not agree about which route to take and we parted. Actually, as I heard after we had arrived in Estonia, the route Mr Vaino took was a better one and they arrived several months earlier in Estonia than we did.

My mother's health deteriorated both emotionally and physically. Because of the Revolution she had lost contact with all her family and relatives. Her mother, who was imprisoned in the labour camp in Saratov had perished from starvation. She had also lost contact with her sister Laura, who was in the USA. Contact with friends or relatives abroad was strictly forbidden because they were 'enemies of the people' and 'traitors'. You could be severely punished if you disobeyed this order.

Mother was also worried about us children because there was nobody else who could look after us. Also, her physical health was poor because of dysentery caused by poor nutrition. And she found travelling in a wagon very difficult. She could not stand the strong shaking of the wagon.

As for me, I did not feel any hardships at all. The month of August was approaching and our food reserves had diminished. In order to survive, we had to beg from the peasants. They were quite kind, especially when we children had to beg. I hated it. And sometimes I stood a long time before I plucked up my courage to knock on the door. But when a friendly old peasant woman asked what I wanted, I felt so relieved that I would be able to bring some food back for the family.

On August 8 my birthday arrived and I was excited. I was now seven years old but I felt quite grown up. As a present I received one teaspoon of sugar. But never had sugar tasted so good! My mother also gave me a ball of wool. I even remember the colour of it – light green. Then she produced a knitting needle and taught me to crochet.

Then trouble struck when two policemen stopped us and asked Father where he was going. My parents must have been very worried because if they had found out that the certificate had been falsified, Father would have been punished or even shot. Yes, this was the horrible Russian Civil War. It could have been the end of us and our escape to Estonia.

They asked for the certificate and told us to follow them to the police station. They were surprised that we had been on our way for nearly four months and that Shamil and Mary were still going strong. They also said that they would get in touch with the Manganese Mine Management near Nikopol. They told Father that the route he had taken was wrong.

At the police station they allowed Mother to sleep in the wagon because she was so ill. Father and we children were put into a police cell. But we were allowed to move freely around the police station. I did not find life in the police station bad in any way except for the food. I remember the lunch which was put before us – tiny dried fish mixed with worms. I could not eat this!

The horses and Mother were glad that the wagon stood still now and they could have a rest. Father slept on the bed which stood on the floor and we children got a bunk. I slept in the upper bunk and Evald and Pavlik in the lower one. We slept on wooden boards with no mattress or sheets and there were no pillows.

I had no trouble with sleep except that at night I heard a strange noise, as if something was falling or being thrown to the ground. After a thorough search we found that the falling objects were apples that were falling from a large tree that stood in the small neglected garden. There were apples just beneath my window. How I craved for an apple! Next morning I asked the Police Commandant if I could have some fallen apples and was glad when he allowed us to gather the fallen apples.

There were two Commandants as we called them. One wore a blue jacket and was called by us 'The Blue Commandant'. And the other had a green jacket and was called 'The Green Commandant'.

Both were quite nice to us, especially when they found that Father was a good chess player. They had seen Father teaching us children to play chess and then started to play chess with Father. Chess is a very popular game in Russia.

Both Commandants found that Father was quite a harmless person and they treated us quite well. Weeks passed and we were not allowed to continue our journey. Apparently because they did not receive any reply from the Manganese Mines. But no wonder, there was a turbulent Civil War going on in Russia.

Our mother had recovered a bit and could make little walks around the place. I remember so well how she walked with us along the large cabbage fields. The air was saturated with the smell of cabbage. Since we were always so hungry, we ate some and found that the taste was not too bad.

Father was very keen to continue our journey since it was autumn now and the cold and the rain would delay it because of the very bad roads and us not having enough warm clothing and blankets. He begged the commandants to let us go. And to my very great surprise they agreed. In fact, they were extremely nice and said they would give us a soldier on horseback who would protect us. They also told us the shortest route to Estonia via Leningrad, which at that moment was in a desperate crisis of famine.

Three

And so we started on the last leg of our escape. Father was glad that no reply had arrived from the Manganese Mines. The certificate falsified by Father was handed back to him and we set off. The soldier was a nice and helpful chap. He even somehow managed to obtain some food for us.

I must tell you, my dear, dear daughters, Astrid, Dagmar and Laura, about another little incident when we had to travel through a large forest. We were very hungry and Father said that he would gather some tasty mushrooms in the forest and then cook them.

We could not wait. Father lit a fire and put the mushrooms in a pot with water. When they were cooked and we started eating them we had to spit them out of our mouths very quickly, they were so bitter. We were so disappointed. I can never forget how disappointed we were. Actually, it must have been a good thing that we spat them out because they must have been poisonous.

My mother had never seen a forest before, because at the Black Sea in the Ukraine there were no forests, only Steppes, with long grass and bushes. And now when we passed through forests she saw birch trees with their white barks and she was so delighted.

Evald, Paul and I were glad when we suddenly saw a little stray dog running behind our wagon. The soldier tried to chase him away but he would not listen and ran after the wagon. I do not know how he survived.

Then eventually we reached Leningrad. It was a dead city. There was a famine crisis. Dead horses were lying in the streets and the starving were cutting meat from their bodies to satisfy their hunger.

Father drove the wagon into a quiet street and went with us children into the Estonian Embassy. Sick Mother stayed in the wagon.

Estonia had been occupied by the Russians but it got its independence in 1918 and was now rid of the Russians. The

Estonian Embassy was a beautiful building and the interior was very impressive with a red carpet on the stairs. I was very impressed since I had never seen anything like it before.

The Estonian personnel at the Embassy were very kind and helpful and could not believe that we had travelled the distance from the Black Sea to Leningrad in a wagon driven only by two horses and that we had escaped the dangers of the Civil War. We were given warm clothing and blankets because the autumn had arrived and we still had a fair bit to travel to Estonia.

There was not much food available and they gave us only some pea flour. They offered us also a room where we could stay the night and sleep. Father took the pea flour and said he would make us some pancakes. We were so looking forward to eating something but the pancakes were really horrible and we had to go to bed hungry. Mother, too, hated the pancakes.

Next morning we continued our escape but after a while Mother was very sick and in very great pain. The pain was so bad that Mother could not tolerate it and Father had to look for a hospital. After a while he found something that looked like a hospital. It was a very big hall full of female and male patients who were very ill and some were dying and crying loudly. This 'Soviet hospital' had no medicines, not even aspirin, no bandages or cotton wool but there was a bed and she did not need to suffer.

But there was a German Pastor with his wife who comforted the patients and looked after them. They promised that they would look after Mother and asked Father for his address in Estonia so that they could write to him about the situation. And so we had to leave Mother with heavy hearts and tears. She seemed to be semi-conscious. We feared we would never see her again.

It was now the end of September and we were approaching the Estonian border. The weather had turned wet and cold. We would probably need several weeks to reach Estonia. Shamil and Mary seemed to look tired and so were all of us.

We were so homesick for the warm Ukraine. I remember how envious I was when I saw a girl in school uniform walking on the street. And I thought how tired I was, sitting for months and months in the wagon. And I missed Mother! Father had enough to do with the driving of the wagon and looking after Shamil and Mary. We were short of food, for ourselves and for the horses.

As we got nearer to the Estonian border we found camps for travelling refugees where we got some food. But on one occasion, Father had forgotten to put down our names for food and we were so hungry.

After weeks we arrived at the frontier. I noticed a big board with the inscription in Russian: 'Proletarians of all nations unite.'

There was soon great activity and everybody talking in Estonian which I did not understand. Our stray dog Rex was the first to jump over the frontier. I was puzzled about one Estonian word being mentioned many times in Father's conversation with the Estonian men. The word was 'palka', 'stick' in Russian and 'wages' in Estonian. I assumed Father was talking about the prospects of getting a job.

After Father had presented his papers we were allowed to pass over the frontier. I was surprised to see so many reporters and photographers. They all wanted to know of the details of our miraculous escape from the Russian Revolution and the Civil War. And how we had managed to travel the long journey which took six months using only two horses.

Father's brother Edward, called Edi, had come to meet us. I was glad to see that he had a big case of food for us. Uncle Edi lived with his parents, my grandparents, in a farm in Kuritsa in the middle of Estonia. It took us several hours to reach it.

Four

At last we were home. Grandmother Elsa and Grandfather Jaan gave us such a great welcome. And we children were greeting them with 'Tere, tere vanaema ja vanaisa.' ('Welcome, welcome, Granny and Grandpa'). How happy were we children to leave now the wagon! And Shamil and Mary got lots of oats and water and a comfortable place in the stable. And we too had comfortable beds and a cosy home.

But we worried about poor Mother. We felt so relieved that we no longer had to worry about our life. Life was so normal here and so peaceful. Granny made me a nice dress. And we had such a nice bath in the sauna. Here every farm had its own sauna and instead of a flannel we used bunches of birch leaves which had a wonderful scent.

How different was life here from life in the Ukraine! The people were more reserved than those in the happy Ukraine. The Estonians are a brother nation of the Finns. The language of both is similar.

I and my brothers had no difficulty with the Estonian language. I must tell you something funny. Evald, Paul and I were walking behind a very old woman. She had a cow on a rope which was eating grass at the road side. We were laughing and singing a little Russian song. She knew we were newcomers learning Estonia. Suddenly she turned round and praised us for singing such a good Estonian song!

Father left Evald, Paul and me with our grandparents and went to Tartu, the second largest city in Estonia, to find a job. He returned after a couple of weeks and said that he and a good friend were to start a motor repair company in Tartu. He also brought good news about Mother's recovery and that he would soon go to Russia to collect her. We were so happy.

We now had the Russian Revolution and the Civil War behind us. But I must point out that I have described it only from my own experience as a girl of seven. My parents must have experienced many more hardships than I have mentioned. I have avoided describing all the terror and the atrocities that took place during the Revolution and the Civil War.

A new episode had started in my life. Estonia was so different from the Ukraine. Evald, Paul and I stayed for nine months at our grandparents'. Father now worked in Tartu and my mother was now in a hospital in Tartu. She had recovered almost completely but was very weak and thin. The doctors at the hospital demonstrated Mother to the students and said that this was an example of how poor the hospitals in Communist Russia were.

Father had rented a flat in Tartu and when my mother was better she would move there, but in the meantime we children still stayed at grandmother's until the winter had passed. Evald, Paul and I loved the winter because there was so much snow. Grandfather took us out in it almost every day in the big farm sledge and Shamil and Mary pulled the sledge so fast over the deep snow that it felt like we were flying.

But on one occasion Evald, Paul and I, although we were tied to the sledge, fell out into the deep snow and Grandfather had to look for some time before he found us. It must have been quite funny. But I was quite frightened because we were all tied together and we could not move.

Granny was busy knitting socks, gloves and jumpers for us from the wool from her sheep. She had a big loom in her bed room and she also wove blankets with nice, bright patterns for us. She also wove material for the men's suits. I thought she was very clever. The rye bread that she made was delicious with her homemade butter.

When spring came we moved to Tartu and at last our family was now together. How nice it was to have Mother with us! When we went out shopping it was so peaceful, she could hardly believe that it was all over. We were delighted to enter a café and to be served with coffee and cakes.

But there was still a problem remaining from our harsh

life. We children got scabies all over our bodies. It was very nasty. We went to a private room in the sauna and Mother put some black, nasty smelling ointment all over us. Thank goodness, we soon got over it.

Autumn was approaching and Mother had to think about a school for us three kids. She chose a German (Baltic German) school because she wanted a school of a larger nation than Estonia and definitely not a Russian school because she had had enough of communist Russia. There was only one Baltic German school. There were no English or French schools.

The first foreign language at the Baltic German school was English. Then came Latin and Russian but not French. I must say that it was a good school because all subjects were taken up to university level.

All three of us kids did well at school and got 'cum laudes'. There was a custom in Estonia that the two best pupils and the Direktor of the school received an invitation from the President of Estonia. At my time the President was Konstatin Pats. I think he was deported with General Laidoner when Russia again occupied Estonia and he died a terrible death.

After finishing school and before going to university I had a gap year. I worked in the Observatory in Tartu and it was very interesting. The Director of the Observatory (which was famous in the Baltic States) was the eminent astronomer Professor Ernst Opik.

Professor Opik was an Estonian astronomer and his grandson Lembit is, at the time I am writing, an MP for the Liberal Party. His grandfather discovered an asteroid that is named after him and Professor Opik also said that an asteroid would collide with planet Earth.

Professor Opik was famous internationally and the University of Harvard in the USA had asked him to take part in an investigation which involved an investigation between the speed and light of shooting stars. For this investigation a large observatory was built and the stars were observed.

Professor Opik had to organize a team of ten who would take part in the calculations. This was printed in the paper and I applied. The applicants had to pass tests and ten of them were selected. I was lucky to be one of them.

A sad incident happened during this work which upset us all. One member of the calculation team was a deaf girl, a very nice girl called Aphrodite Rosenthal. She was dismissed on the spot by a manager because she was laughing and talking when she was supposed to be working. She was so upset that she went home and hanged herself in the attic. The whole team stopped work on this day.

After the gap year was over I prepared to study medicine at the University of Tartu. We had to pass entrance exams in Latin, Physics, Chemistry, Botany and Zoology. Most of the professors at the university lectured in Russian. This was a bit confusing. (*While at university as a medical student, my mother met my father, Bruno Lustig, who was a medical student a couple of years ahead of her. They met during a lecture given by the Nobel prize winning physicist Max Planck.*)

My brother Evald wanted to study road and bridge engineering and building but there were no colleges for this in Estonia. Father suggested that he should study in Germany and he went to Hannover and got a good degree.

Five

Usually we spent our summer holidays at our grandparents' farm. This was wonderful! The farm was surrounded by many forests and since there had been no forests near our house in the Ukraine this was new to us. It was a great attraction to explore these large Estonian forests. They mainly consisted of fir and pine trees and also birch trees.

In summer the forests were full of wild strawberries, blackberries, raspberries and cranberries and we collected them by the bucketful. We preserved them either in bottles for the winter or made jam. At that time there was no jam in the shops.

Father insisted that we always had sticks in case of snakes. Sometimes we did see them and we killed them. We then put the snakes on large ant hills so that the ants would eat them. Later we would see that all of the flesh had gone and only the skeletons were left.

One summer day when Grandfather was driving us in his cart to the farm I saw that one forest close to the farm had completely disappeared. It had been cut down. I was so shocked. I had loved this forest most of all. It was a forest of beautiful large pine trees. I cried and cried and my heart ached so much.

I was very attached to nature, to trees, forests, fields and meadows full of lovely flowers. I remember the mushrooms we used to collect, early in the morning, around five a.m., yellow and red mushrooms. They looked so beautiful, growing in the green moss.

I did not need any company. I so liked walking along the little path where the air was scented with white clover blossoms and the potato field was like a large flower bed. And the rye field, full of blue rye flowers!

But most attractive of all was the blue flax field in bloom. It looked like a cloud that had descended to the earth from heaven. In the autumn Grandma and I pulled the flax out and arranged it into bundles and them immersed it in a little pool of water.

I have forgotten the whole procedure, but I saw Grandma spinning the threads and weaving sheets and towels. The sheets were a bit rough when you slept in them. She embroidered the family monogram on the towels with red thread. Grandma also spun the the wool from her own sheep and she knitted socks and jumpers and wove blankets and material for men's suits.

I admired her so much. She got up in the summer at four a.m. and helped the shepherd boy to take the cows and sheep to the grazing fields. The shepherd boy was hired for the whole summer. Half of his pay was money and the rest was a sack of potatoes, flour, butter, and the material for a suit.

My dear Astrid, Dagmar and Laura, I hope you are not bored with the detailed descriptions of your ancestors. But to me they are all very dear and I think of them quite often, especially Grandmother Elsa. I shall tell you more about Grandmother. I must mention that she never cleaned the windows. But there were many flies and the windows were very much in need of a good cleanup. When I asked her why she did not clean the windows, she said, oh, they will soon be dirty again. (In saying this, I don't mean it in a bad way but I thought her excuse was really rather funny.)

But the next day I saw her going into the forest and coming back with some beautiful but poisonous mushrooms. She put them on a plate, sprinkled them with sugar and poured some water over them. Soon I saw dead flies lying all over the table.

When Grandma ironed, she put lots of burning coals from the oven into the iron. But the burning bits of coal fell out and spoilt the clothes because the iron was broken. Yes, her life was not easy.

I liked to go with Grandma to the edge of the forest to cut long juicy grass from the earth. The way the sunset transformed the evening light in the forest was fascinating. And it was so peaceful, as if the forest was preparing to sleep.

Now I am going to describe my Grandpa Jaan. My Grandpa Jaan was a very happy and sociable man. Unfortunately some time ago a horse had given him a hefty kick on the nose and his nose was disfigured. It was in the shape of a rose and he could not breathe through his nostrils. But he seemed to manage very well. He was always asked to officiate at funerals and weddings because he was so sociable and he had a good singing voice. He also liked a drink very much.

My uncle Edi was also very sociable. My mother gave him her guitar which she had brought from the Ukraine and he could play it very well, although he had never been taught. He liked shooting deer in the forest and got into trouble with the law when he did not observe the time when it was forbidden to shoot them.

He was so angry with the policeman who made him pay a fine that when he saw the policeman in the pub he threw a fish into his face. The pub was so full of people and nobody noticed who the culprit was. And so he got away with it.

When we were on holiday at my grandparents' farm my brothers and I liked to sleep in the attic on the hay. The hay was so soft and fragrant. Grandpa had his tobacco leaves which he had growing there and also bunches of birches for the sauna. For us children, Grandpa's farm was a real paradise.

And I remember how once, when I was walking in the fields, I thought how lucky we were to possess this land and that it would always be there and one day it would be ours. But I was wrong. During the Second World War the land was confiscated by the Russians who had once again occupied Estonia. Collective farming was introduced.

Still worse, my grandmother, my grandfather and Uncle Edi were deported to Siberia and died there a horrible death. When we fled from Estonia as the Russians were approaching, we tried to persuade them to come with us. But they would not hear of it. They said they would never leave their land. Uncle Edi said he would join the Forest

Brothers and live in the forest. My grandma was an old lady and had never hurt anyone. And I hate to think how upset she must have been to leave all her dear cattle behind. (*Both grandparents were in their seventies and it is unlikely that they even survived the harsh and degrading journey in cattle trucks filled to capacity.*)

My family and I escaped narrowly to the West. But I shall tell you more about this later.

War

War

In the interval, my mother has married and had two children. The Russian and Nazi occupations of Estonia have taken place. She has lost both of her brothers in the war. Her grandparents and uncle have been deported to Siberia. Her husband, Bruno, a doctor, has disappeared on the Russian Front.

1944 – Spring 1945: She has fled with her children and parents, first to a friend in Neustatten, East Germany and from there to another friend in Schwerin.

In trying to get to Schwerin, late Spring 1945...

We found that trains were not operating regularly. I remember how we all, including Waldrant and Mother stood on the platform and waited for a train. My girls Astrid and Dagmar were still very young, Astrid about three and Dagmar under a year.

One train passed. It was full of German soldiers fleeing from the Front. Then came another train which did stop and again full of soldiers. People stormed to get in. And I was so worried that we could not make it and that I would become separated from the children. But we made it.

There was hardly even any standing room. One soldier stood up and gave us his seat and another offered sweets to the children. I looked around and saw that the windows of the train were broken. This had probably happened when the Russians had been shooting at the train.

Hours passed and at last we arrived at Schwerin. We were so hungry and cold but Waldrant made us comfortable. A big fire was burning in the kitchen and soon we sat at the kitchen table and ate a hot meal. The house was very large and sleeping facilities were found for everyone.

We were told that the house had a funeral office *(I believe the family that we were staying with were undertakers.).* When my mother heard this she smiled and said 'How convenient'. I remember these words because they upset me.

My poor, dear mother died after two days. She had severe pneumonia. A doctor did prescribe tablets, but they did not help. She suffered badly, becoming unconscious. She hallucinated and turned a nasty yellow in colour and she closed her eyes forever. Ingrid's Aunt Brigitte was very helpful and very sympathetic. I went out to buy lily of the valley flowers, her favourite flowers, but I could not get any. I returned to find that Aunt Brigitte had got some.

The funeral service was very touching with a priest and a quartet of musicians and I felt such a pain in my heart that I thought I would faint. The cemetery was quite close and my father and I and Ingrid's aunt followed the coffin to the grave. It was a cold day but the sun had come out and that was comforting.

The next day I went to visit her grave. But there had been bombing during the night. A bomb had fallen on her grave and it was unrecognisable.

We were coming towards the end of the war. Then Schwerin was taken by the English army. I remember standing at the window and waving to them. Oh, we were so happy! I spoke to an English army Padre and told him that my family wanted to go to England and from there to the States. But he thought that we would have to be a little patient.

A couple of days later I happened to be at the Post Office and I met an Estonian family, the Oinases. They said that the next day they were going to a camp for displaced persons from the Baltic. This sounded like a God sent message to me. The Estonian family told me what time and where to meet them the next morning. We would then have to walk for a few hours to get to the camp.

My father welcomed the news. But there was one problem. Little Dagmar could not walk for that distance. Ingrid's aunt gave us a little cart that her son had used when he was a baby. We had to walk for about seven hours and we had to rest a lot.

The displaced Baltic refugees were housed in a large German factory consisting of several large buildings. We were so tired and were so glad of the nice welcome we got and the comfortable accommodation and the food. I was thinking how lucky we were to have got to know about this just by chance. The English army looked after us well and the Americans regularly sent large parcels of high quality food.

Since most of the displaced refugees from the Baltic could not speak English, I got the job of teaching them every day. People were very keen to learn and I was paid quite handsomely. Father also got a job as an engineer, for which he was paid.

There were even soldiers posted to guard the camp, although the war was over. The camp was quite near Hamburg. (*in Schwarzenbeck*).

All went well in the camp but my little Dagmar got suddenly very ill. The camp doctor took her immediately to the hospital in Hamburg. She got good treatment and recovered after a few weeks. (*I believe the illness was meningitis*).

After about a year, we were told that hospitals in England did not have enough nurses and nurses from the Baltic States would be welcomed. They would be well paid, would have free travel to England and the contract would be for at least a year. (*I think this was called the Baltic Swans project*).

I thought that this would be a good opportunity to get to England and then from there to go to the States. I worried about leaving Astrid and Dagmar with Father but I felt that this was a good opportunity and so I volunteered. Quite a large number had put themselves forward for this. I hated leaving Astrid and Dagmar for a year and thought for a long time how to get out of this. But there just was no way out.

Then came the time when we had to depart for London. The ship was quite comfortable but we had to sleep in

41

hammocks. I was glad the sea was quite calm.

In London we were taken to the Estonian Embassy where we were given clothes and pocket money. Then the staff of the embassy took us on a double-decker bus for a tour of London. Then we had a nice meal. The first thing I bought in London was a big bunch of grapes. It was such a treat because we did not have grapes in Estonia or Germany.

After this we were allocated to different hospitals. I had hoped to be allocated to a hospital in London and was a bit disappointed to be allocated to Papworth Hospital near Cambridge. It was a hospital for patients with TB and cardiac diseases. We had very comfortable accommodation in two nurses' homes.

The work was not demanding. I was put on night duty and was pleased that the salary was higher than the day wages. We were photographed and the pictures appeared in a Cambridge newspaper. I regularly sent parcels to father and Astrid and Dagmar. I missed them and time seemed to creep so slowly.

I got to know the wife of a Professor of Physiology who visited the hospital. She often took me to Cambridge and showed me the colleges. I was very impressed by King's College. She invited me for meals at her house and also took me out to restaurants.

I was surprised one day to get a nice letter. It was from my Edinburgh pen pal William Gillis with whom I had been corresponding for several years because I wanted to improve my English. (He had sent me many English books to Estonia and said that he wanted to visit me in Estonia.) He had been trying to get in touch with me during the war but had not succeeded.

I replied immediately and he came to visit me in Papworth Hopsital. He had finished his studies at Edinburgh University (*In Divinity*) and he had been ordained. He was looking for a parish in Scotland.

At that time he was living with his mother in Edinburgh. We became good friends. Soon after this, he wrote that the Church of Scotland had given him a parish in Foss, near

Pitlochry, Perthshire. His mother was going to sell their house and would move to Foss with him.

After they had moved to Foss they invited me for a holiday, which I gladly accepted. Foss Manse was a very large impressive building, built in 1767 of beautiful stone. My friend William's mother had had it beautifully furnished with the money that she received for her three storey house in Edinburgh. She had bought mahogany furniture and expensive carpets from Jenner's in Princes Street.

I was very impressed with everything, but most of all with the Scottish Highlands, the beautiful hills, forests, the heather and the lochs. Everything was so beautiful and so peaceful. The Highlands had not suffered from the war. I felt I was in paradise.

I remember the first day of the holiday so clearly. The sun was shining. William and I walked past the brook which supplied the manse with water, which, as I found out later, was so soft and aromatic. We walked up the hill to the Cameron's farm to get milk.

William introduced me to the school teacher, Miss Robertson. The school was opposite the small church and had four pupils. I found her very charming. She lived with her mother in the school house. She had been engaged but could not marry because her mother wanted her completely for herself and she obeyed her mother in this.

William asked me how I liked Papworth Hospital and enquired about my father and two little girls in the camp. He asked if I had had any letters from Bruno, my husband. I said that I had not heard from him for over four years.

The holiday at the manse was very pleasant. William, his mother and I went to Pitlochry and Aberfeldy for meals and the food was superb. In the afternoons we sat in the spring sunshine in the garden and had afternoon tea with short bread. There was a large rhododendron bush with red blooms beside the gate and in the distance the wooded hills. It was so beautiful. It seemed like a beautiful dream after all the horror and destruction that I had experienced on the Continent, especially the loss of so many members of my family: my grandparents, uncle, brothers, mother and husband.

On the evening before my departure William and I were sitting in his study and listening to music. William suddenly asked me if I would like to marry him. I must admit that I was expecting this. I was very happy.

When I returned from my holiday, I told Matron and Staff the news and they congratulated me. And of course a letter was sent to Father and my girls.

The wedding took place in a church in Edinburgh where William had served as a minister. The best man was a lecturer in Greek at Edinburgh University. The reception was held at a hotel in Edinburgh.

My next problem was to bring my father and girls to Scotland. William said he was looking forward to meeting the girls and that he liked their names, Astrid and Dagmar. I booked a flight to Hamburg. I could not wait to see my dear ones.

There was a stormy reunion when I arrived at the camp. The camp now had a smaller number of Baltic refugees. They could not return to their homeland because the Soviets were still there. Gradually they disappeared to different countries such as Canada and America.

I and my family departed the next day by train. Unfortunately we had a nasty experience when we wanted to pass through Holland. The man who checked our certificates said that I and the girls could go through but my father could not because he did not have the appropriate papers. Father would have to travel back to the camp to fetch them. I could not believe it. This meant all of us would have to go back to the camp.

No argument helped. I said Father was an old man and would not harm anyone and that we did not intend to stay in Holland but only to pass through it. No, it is not possible, he said. So back we went. Father got his papers and we started our journey to Scotland.

William met us at Pitlochry station, helped us with all our bundles and drove us to Foss Manse. The atmosphere was very happy and William's mother had cooked a meal for us. I was glad to see that William loved the kids and they loved him and his mother loved them too.

Astrid and Dagmar soon felt as if they were in their own home. They explored the big house, the garden and the surroundings. I had prepared their room and also one for Father. There was no language barrier.

The next day I went with my kids to Foss School. Miss Robertson was the only teacher for all grades of pupil. And she was glad to have Astrid and Dagmar because she then had six pupils to teach. She was a very good teacher and Astrid and Dagmar had no difficulties at all. Astrid was six years old and Dagmar three and a half.

At that time there was a Hydro-electric Scheme at Tummel Bridge and the River Tummel, which ran close by the manse, was transformed into a loch. It was a great event. I remember how the river gradually swelled in size and moved into the surrounding meadows. And the life of all the animals was endangered. Little rabbits were running for their lives. It was so sad. Loch Tummel is now quite close to the manse.

About two years pass. An important event has taken place but my mother does not talk about it. It is now summer, 1949...

I was expecting a baby and I wanted the local doctor to examine me. He came from Kinloch Rannoch, examined me and said that I was not pregnant. He was wrong and I was sure that I was. I had noticed that this doctor frequently made wrong diagnoses. The district nurse knew more than he did.

Time passed and I felt that the baby would be delivered soon. One night at about midnight I fell into labour and asked my father to run to the post office to phone for the district nurse. We had no phone at the manse. Father was so excited that he did not stop to put his shoes on but ran in only his socks to the post office. *(over a mile away)*

Meanwhile I was lying in bed feeling the baby being born and all of a sudden it was there without any help. But no nurse had come. I waited and waited and then I took the scissors from my dressing table and cut the umbilical cord myself. The nurse arrived later, changed the bed clothes and bathed and dressed the baby.

For some reason the baby, whom we called Laura after my favourite aunt, was restless at night. I used to take her out of her basket and walk for hours around the bedroom to get her to sleep but she would not respond.

Christmas was coming and I had to start cleaning the large house. Baby Laura was still crying in her basket during the day. I could not understand why this was. Then I thought that the reason might be a ghost. I had had some bad experiences and little Dagmar did, too. One evening she had come to tell me that supper was ready. Suddenly someone gripped her from behind and turned her upside down and then let her go and silently vanished. *(Despite my incredulity, Dagmar always maintained that someone had picked her up, turned her upside down and then put her down.)*

I learnt later that there had indeed been bad experiences in the past connected to the manse and sometimes workmen had refused to enter the manse. One theory is that some nuns had lived on this spot in the past and they had been murdered by Sassenachs (the English). It appeared that the evil spirit was in my bedroom. *(Foss Church was founded in 625 AD by St Chad and it is quite possible that a religious community had lived on the site of the manse.)*

Apart from this, life proceeded happily. I was so happy to be there after all the horrors of the war. In summer there were masses of swallows flying around the manse. A swift also had a nest outside my window. The garden outside my window was so beautiful. There was a bush with a wonderful scent outside my window. In the summer there were wonderful golden sunsets. It was so peaceful, with the swallows flying around the manse.

The Scourge of Tongues

There is a certain bleakness in my mother's description at the end of this last section in which she describes the birth of my sister Laura. She seems to be alone. Why? Where was William? Is it really possible that she had come to full term without any medical help? She could have lost her life while giving birth alone in an isolated manse.

The answer is that there has been an event that has changed everything. My father, Bruno Lustig, about whom nothing had been heard for six years, had come back, as it were, from the dead. He had indeed vanished after three months on the Russian Front but his fate had been that he had been taken to a concentration camp close to the border with Estonia. He had finally been released by the Soviet authorities. He had gone to Germany and was now looking for his family.

His sudden appearance was a great shock on many levels, emotional and legal. From a legal point of view it was of course bigamy. However, it was not bigamy in the 'normal' sense in that the circumstances around it were far from normal. It was in fact a common situation after World War Two, so common that the usual decision of a court was that there were no guilty parties. This is what happened in my mother's case when it was heard in the Court at Lubeck in Germany. She was told, simply, that she had only to choose which husband she wished to remain with.

This in itself must have presented my mother with dreadful emotional pressures. She decided to remain with William and, since her life had, for the past six years, been away from her normal married life in Estonia, it seems to me to have been a logical decision. There had been so much insecurity in her life that she must have craved, for once in her life, to feel secure.

However, as we shall soon see – security was not a fate destined for her.

To repeat: in legal terms, my mother was seen to be

blameless and her union with William was not in any way compromised. Certain formalities would have to be undertaken. She would have to obtain a divorce from my father and then she would have to undergo another marriage ceremony with William. But these were seen as mere formalities.

So: the courts accepted the situation. As for the Church of Scotland, it too saw this tragic event as yet more fallout from a terrible war. It did not allocate any blame to my mother, or to William. Their marriage could continue and William's ministry at Foss could continue.

So: they lived happily ever after? No: there was another twist to an already painful situation.

I had always imagined that there would be lurid headlines in the local papers about this awful situation. I thought there would be a 'News of the World' style of story about a local minister and his foreign wife and I only quite recently had the courage to trawl through newspaper reports of the period. I was surprised to find that there was only a very brief notice in the Dundee Courier for April 3, 1950. It said only that the Rev'd W.A.C. Gillis had offered his resignation from his post as minister of Foss Kirk and that his resignation had been accepted.

If the Church of Scotland accepted that the situation was normal and without blame and that William could continue in his ministry at Foss, why did he have to present his resignation? William loved the Highlands. His family, or, to go back in time, his clan, the Campbells, had come from a Highland area quite close to Perthshire and he had always longed for a parish in the Highlands.

My mother told me the whole story only when I was older and more able to understand the situation. She told me that the parishioners of Foss and Tummel had been unable to accept the situation. They could not accept William's ministry, the ministry of someone who, in their eyes, was compromised. In their view, my mother was not innocent. I suppose that is what they thought. Actually, I have no idea what they thought. The main fact is that they expressed their feelings in a very clear way. As an entire body, they stopped attending church.

In fact, I can remember this. For some time my mother and I were the only people to attend church. It did not strike me – I was only seven at the time – that anything was wrong. Sunday after Sunday, the two of us sat in the front pew and looked up at Daddy while he preached and conducted the service. I don't remember thinking this was odd in any way and I don't remember wondering where the other parishioners were. I just thought, as I had come to accept so many unusual things, that this was how life was.

My mother also told me that the Church of Scotland was 'furious' with the parishioners and, as a reaction, sold the manse and stripped the Parish of Foss and Tummel of a dedicated minister. From then on, Foss Kirk was to be combined with the Parish Church of Kinloch Rannoch.

I think the word 'furious' perhaps expresses my mother's feelings rather than that of the Church of Scotland. I have not looked into Church of Scotland records regarding this situation, and of course I do not have any knowledge of how decisions were made and how events proceeded, but of course there must have been meetings and certain conclusions must have been arrived at. For whatever reasons, the manse was accordingly sold and the Parish of Foss and Tummel was combined with the Parish of Kinloch Rannoch, as indeed it is today.

Before this happened, the Church of Scotland had quickly removed William from the parish and had appointed him to the post of Chaplain to the Seaforth Highlanders, who at that time were posted abroad. This explains his absence from the manse at the time of his daughter's birth.

As I try to recreate the time line of events with a view to seeing how things unfolded, I think that my father's letter must have arrived in the spring or early summer of 1949. William must have joined the Seaforth Highlanders between then and November 1949. His resignation was considered and accepted by the Elders of the church at a meeting in Aberfeldy on 30 March 1950 and we finally left the manse in late 1950. It now seems a very long time for us to remain in a hostile situation, but remain we did.

I was only seven and not properly aware of what was happening in the community. Dagmar and I still played in the beautiful surroundings of the manse. We wandered through the moors and little woods surrounding the manse and met nobody. We went to school as normal. Daddy was no longer there – some explanation must have been given to us. The 'scandal', as I suppose it was seen by the community, was not mentioned to us. Perhaps there were certain overtones in the way we were treated at school by the parents of the other pupils who had also stopped attending church. If so, I did not notice.

However, looking back and reading between the lines, it is clear that my moother was, effectively, ostracised. Her husband was no longer the minister. Nobody visited the manse or communicated with her. This explains why nobody knew that she was pregnant, my sister's birth being yet another shock for the community.

After Laura was born my mother suffered a nervous breakdown and spent some time at the Cottage Hospital in Aberfeldy. We were then greatly helped by Kitty and William Brown, who lived in Tummel Bridge. They remained friends long after we had left Foss. Their daughter Margaret, who was at the village school with her sister Elizabeth, is still a friend today.

With William abroad, we stayed at the manse until arrangements had been made for us to move to new accommodation. Again, I have no idea why this should have taken so long. Eventually we were moved to the Officers' Quarters in Redford Barracks, Colinton, Edinburgh, where the Seaforth Highlanders were stationed.

Visualise the scenario then, in mid November 1949. My mother is alone, in an advanced state of pregnancy. I remember that night very well. It was a wild November night, with the wind whistling through the windows and the rain beating against the window panes. Dagmar and I were sleeping in the bedroom that overlooked the front door. It was very dark.

We were awakened by screams. It was my mother in a state of labour but we did not know this. We did not know what to do. I would normally have run through to my mother's bedroom but the screams were quite terrifying. I thought she was being murdered. Then the thought struck me that we would be next and I burrowed deeper into my bed.

We lay there for what seemed like an eternity, with the wind and the rain lashing against the window. Then I heard voices, and a woman's voice as well as my grandfather's. I still did not know what to do. The screams had ceased. Was my mother now dead and the police had come to view the body?

I stiffened as I heard footsteps coming towards our door – but some instinct told me that things were not so bad. Then the light went on and a smiling face, a face belonging to the district nurse, looked at us cowering in our beds.

'You have a baby sister,' she said.

Dagmar and I got out of bed and went through to my mother's bedroom. There she was, a tiny baby, lying in a Moses basket. We stared at her. I had not thoughts at all about my mother, who was lying in the bed beside the Moses basket. Dagmar and I went back to our bedroom.

My Father

My father, Bruno Lustig, was taken prisoner on the Russian Front. He was then placed in a concentration camp close to the Estonian border. He survived only because he was a doctor. He was put to work in the camp infirmary and his living conditions were therefore marginally better than that of the other prisoners. His life was spared also because he had performed an operation on the camp Commandant which had saved his life. Almost everybody else in that concentration camp perished.

On his release, my father moved to the south of Germany and he married again. He pursued a distinguished career as a psychiatrist in a large psychiatric hospital. I find it interesting to think that he was treating patients but it never occurred to him to seek help for his experience in the concentration camp, or for the loss of his family. That is of course true of all the men who fought in the war. They came home, said nothing, carried on as normal.

The hospital in which my father worked was one of the largest, if not the largest, state psychiatric hospitals in Germany. It was based in the Abbey of Schussenried, a huge, sprawling abbey dating from 1183 AD. Today it is a museum, both as an important Christian monument and as a Centre of Psychiatry, part of the University of Ulm, showcasing the work that went on in the healing of those suffering from psychiatric illnesses. It is indeed a magnificent building. The large library, with its beautiful ceiling, must be one of the most impressive in Europe.

I remember standing there with Dagmar on our first visit to our father. We were quite young but he did not spare us. From the beauty of the library he showed us round the rest of the hospital. We visited an outside yard where several patients – he described them as 'manic' – were energetically hewing wood. Inside the hospital there were all sorts of workshops for arts and crafts. In one of the surgical wards, we were shown an anaesthetized patient lying in a cot and being treated with electro-convulsive therapy.

As well as working in the hospital in Schussenried, my father acted as a forensic psychiatrist for the government, often assessing criminals such as murderers to see whether they were clinically insane or not.

During the 1950s my father was approached by the World Health Organisation. There was world- wide concern over the so-called 'psychiatric hospitals' in the Soviet Union. These hospitals were people by political dissidents. In the Soviet Union disagreement with the political status quo was regarded as a mental illness. The heavy medication with which these 'patients' were treated led quickly to an early death.

My father was the only psychiatrist in the world who satisfied both the criteria of the medical establishment in the West and that of the Soviet Union. This was because, as an Estonian, the Soviets perceived him as belonging to them (they had at that time occupied Estonia and claimed it as their own) and of course he was a practising psychiatrist in the West.

He spent many months researching the hospitals and interviewing the patients. In the official report that followed he said that the inmates of the hospitals were not mentally ill. He was then made *persona non grata* by the Soviet authorities and he was barred from entering Russia.

My father's published research was well received by the medical profession. His book, 'Soviet Psychiatry', published in 1955, was on the amazon website until quite recently.

A Memory of Foss, Christmas 1947

I don't think I shall ever forget my first Christmas at Foss Manse when I was six years old. It was such a contrast to the Christmases I had spent with my grandfather at the refugee camp in Germany.

The camp, as I remember it, was a bleak place, a huge red brick building surrounded by what seemed like acres and acres of cinders. Go out and play, Grandpa used to say, go out and play. So the two of us used to set off. I can't remember what we played at. I do remember standing in a queue, holding a tin mug and waiting to be served with soup. Quite often, as I walked away clutching my soup, a group of boys used to swoop towards me and then take the mug from my hands.

I can remember one Christmas at the camp.

When is Mummy coming? I asked my grandfather.

She isn't coming.

You said she was coming.

She isn't coming. Sit here and play.

He placed me in front of the table and put two sweets in front of me.

I don't want to play. What can I play at?

Pretend the sweets are sheep. One sheep is the mother and the other sweet is the child. Or pretend one sweet is a sheep and the other is a wolf. There's lots of things you can pretend.

The contrast the following year could not have been greater. Here we were in a large room, in front of a roaring log fire. Beside the fire there was a huge Christmas tree, reaching almost to the ceiling. It was covered in beautiful shining decorations and silver tinsel that sparkled as it picked up the light from the fire. Best of all, it was decorated with a myriad tiny candles, red candles, blue candles, lit up with real flames.

Before this, William had taken us on a trip to Edinburgh, to Jenner's in Princes Street. I suppose it would be fair to equate Jenner's with Harrod's in London. Of course, today I can imagine exactly what William had been thinking although I would not have been aware of this at the time. *These children have been in a refugee camp, they have had very little, now they are my children, I am going to see that they have whatever they want, whatever they want…*

He took us up to the floor where the children's toys were and placed us in front of what seemed like a huge mass of gleaming toys: bicycles, dolls, teddy bears, soft animals, dolls' houses, it all seemed quite endless.

Take what you want, he said, go and take what you want. You can have whatever you want.

Dagmar and I just stood there. I can remember a feeling of nausea sweeping through me. I felt quite paralysed. Neither of us seemed able to move.

Of course, as an adult, I am well able to understand this reaction. After the very plain circumstances of the camp, this vision of plenty was just too much for us to cope with. I believe it is the same when it comes to food. I understand that many refugees, having been used to very plain food for some time, find it difficult to eat rich food. Dagmar, in fact, suffered from a sort of 'materialistic anorexia' all her life, hating anything grand or what to her seemed excessive.

Come on, come on, said William, choose whatever you want…

My mother and William's mother joined in but it was useless. Neither of us could move. In the end we were each given a teddy bear and a doll, chosen by the adults.

Now we were together and it was Christmas Eve and my mother was with me. Grandpa was happy and jolly and William's mother, Christina, was happy too.

It had been snowing heavily. I had never seen snow before, or at least snow like this, huge swirling flakes racing towards the window panes. I felt anxious because Daddy, as I called him, was not there. I hoped that he was not somewhere out there, lost in the snow. When I had asked my mother where he was, she had smiled mysteriously and said nothing.

Then a man in a red suit came charging into the room.

It's Santa Claus! It's Santa Claus! Mummy exclaimed.

I was my usual argumentative self.

No, it isn't. It's Daddy.

My mother put a finger to her lips and pointed to Dagmar.

It's a nice picture: the snow falling in the Highlands, the blazing fire, all of us together and happy.

Photographs

Happy days at Foss Manse:
Astrid (on bench), Dagmar and Estonian friend Tiiu and her
mother, Leida Ojasoo.

My mother

William

My Grandfather

My grandmother Louise, who died in Schwerin, 1945.

My great-grandmother Christine, who died in the concentration camp, Saratov, Russia, 1917.

Front page of the family Bible – when my great-grandmother was married in the Church of St. Peter and St. Paul, Moscow, 1877.

Russian Easter card, 'Christ is Risen', 1913. Sent by my
mother's brother Ewald to his Aunt Laura.

My grandmother's sister Laura.

Myself with my sister Laura.

My father with Dagmar (1943 – 2015)

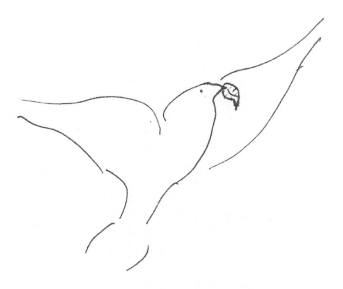

All is calm. The dove, symbol of peace, brings Noah a leaf from an olive tree.

Printed in Great Britain
by Amazon